Brenda

Great to have a 4th year
I wish I had in the house!
Hope you had a great summer
back in *whole*!

All the best

Elin
8/28/19

Written by:
Dan Zadra and
Kobi Yamada

*Where will
you be five years
from today?*

ASK QUESTIONS, MAKE CHOICES, TAKE STEPS—

TODAY IS THE DAY.

Life offers itself to us in an endless number of ways, but we seldom see or accept more than a tiny fraction of the exciting possibilities around us.

The truth is most of us are so busy doing what we think we have to do that we never get around to doing what we really want to do.

You can design your life to come to you the way you want it. You don't have to take life the way it comes to you.

DECIDE WHAT'S NEXT

IN YOUR LIFE AND STRATEGIZE HOW TO GET IT.

This is your life, your one-and-only life. What is it going to be? You decide. Starting today, you can make the next five years the most exciting, satisfying, productive, and amazing years of your life so far—or just another five years.

The purpose of this book is to stir your creative juices and inspire you to get in touch with your dreams. The goal is not to provide a list of what *should* be done with the next five years—but to stir up some exciting possibilities of what *could* be done.

Over the next five years, what do you really want to do? What do you really want to have? Who do you really want to be? Where do you really want to go?

In the following pages, you'll find fresh ways of thinking about different areas of your life. You could do something as significant as trace your roots, bring an exciting idea into the world, pursue a heart-quickening adventure, or think of a creative way to give back.

The truth is you really can turn any *what if?* into *what is.*

DON'T SAY YOU DON'T HAVE ENOUGH TIME.
YOU HAVE EXACTLY THE SAME NUMBER
OF HOURS PER DAY THAT WERE GIVEN TO
HELEN KELLER, PASTEUR, MICHELANGELO,
MOTHER TERESA, LEONARDO DA VINCI,
THOMAS JEFFERSON, AND ALBERT EINSTEIN.

H. JACKSON BROWN JR.

FIVE YEARS...

260 weeks... 1,825 days... 2,628,000 minutes.

It took Michelangelo fewer than five years to paint the Sistine Chapel.

What will you do with it? What *could* you do with it?

In five years, Shakespeare wrote *Hamlet*, *Othello*, *King Lear*, *Macbeth*, and five other plays.

In 1961, Julia Child was an unknown name on the cover of a quirky new cookbook. Five years later, she was America's favorite TV chef and the winner of an Emmy Award.

Fired from their home improvement jobs, Arthur Blank and Bernie Marcus created a business called the Home Depot. Within five years, their annual sales exceeded $250 million.

At age 30, Amazon founder Jeff Bezos was working out of a garage. Five years later, his net worth was almost $10 billion.

Within just five years, entrepreneur Elon Musk helped grow three world-changing companies: PayPal, SpaceX, and Tesla Motors.

"YOU HAVE BRAINS IN YOUR HEAD.
YOU HAVE FEET IN YOUR SHOES. YOU CAN
STEER YOURSELF ANY DIRECTION YOU
CHOOSE. YOU'RE ON YOUR OWN. AND YOU
KNOW WHAT YOU KNOW. AND *YOU* ARE
THE GUY WHO'LL DECIDE WHERE TO GO."

DR. SEUSS

Live your life on purpose:

The best day of your life is the day you decide your life is your own. No one to lean on, rely on, or blame. The gift of life is yours, it is an amazing journey, and you alone are responsible for the quality of it. Life is about the choices you make—choose wisely. Start by choosing the two most important "guiding stars"—your values and your mission.

Choose your values:

Values are personal choices you make about what's important to you. Being guided by your highest values brings immense satisfaction and meaning to life.

Here are some examples of lifetime values:

COMMUNITY FAMILY **FRIENDSHIP** LOVE
CAREER **HEALTH** WEALTH **LEARNING**
ADVENTURE FAITH **INTEGRITY** ART
LEISURE **CREATIVITY** SUSTAINABILITY

HERE ARE SOME QUESTIONS THAT WILL HELP YOU IDENTIFY YOUR

LIFETIME VALUES.

Who are the two people I like and respect the most, and why?

Who is the happiest person I know?

What are the three things I like most and least about myself?

How would I describe myself?

TOP FIVE

LIFETIME VALUES IS A SHORTCUT TO IDENTIFYING YOUR GOALS.

What are *your* top five values?

1

2

3

4

5

CHOOSE YOUR MISSION.

(Your life is worth one!)

Here are examples of how some high-achieving and inspirational people might have worded their own mission statements:

Walt Disney: My mission in life is to make people happy.

Anitra Freeman, artist: I believe creativity is the essence of being human. I believe I make myself, and I won't buy my soul off the rack.

Larry Page and Sergey Brin, founders of Google: Our mission is to make the world's information accessible to everyone.

Rachel Carson, author and conservationist: My life's mission is to share the wonder and beauty of the natural world with people.

Phil Knight, cofounder of Nike: My mission is to bring inspiration and innovation to every athlete in the world.

Shonda Rhimes, producer and screenwriter: I want to tell stories truthfully and without boundaries; to make TV shows that look like the real world does.

WRITE YOUR PERSONAL
MISSION STATEMENT:

There's no specific format for writing your personal mission statement—only you will know how to write it—but try to keep it clear, brief, and exciting. Just ask yourself, "What is my calling, my life's aim? What inspires me the most? What activity or service are my core values urging me to pursue?"

FOLLOW YOUR DREAMS.

THEY
KNOW
THE
WAY.

A GOAL IS A DREAM SET TO PAPER.

Don't just think it—ink it!

It sounds incredible, but according to Dave Kohl, a professor emeritus at Virginia Tech, 80 percent of Americans don't have goals. Approximately 16 percent say they do have goals, but they don't ever write them down. Only 4 percent do write down their goals, and fewer than 1 percent actually review them on an ongoing basis.

DREAMS!

(Look, they just became goals!)

*If you don't have a dream, how
can you have a dream come true?*

Money isn't everything.

Psychologist Ed Diener was researching happiness
and well-being when he made an amazing discovery.
On a scale of one to seven, where one means "not at
all satisfied with my life" and seven means "completely
satisfied," he found that the people on *Forbes* magazine's
list of the 400 richest Americans averaged 5.8. The Maasai
people of Kenya and Tanzania enjoy a semi-nomadic
lifestyle — and ranked almost exactly the same.

BALANCE IS

BEAUTIFUL.

Setting goals in only one or two areas of life is like rowing a boat with only one oar—you go round and round in only one direction. If you use all your creativity in just one area of your life, you are destined to be one-dimensional in others. (What's the use of being a multimillionaire five years from now if your family life suffers?)

THE WHEEL OF
LIFE.

Think of your life as a wheel with many different spokes. To have a balanced life, each spoke needs your attention.

Balance the wheel of your life. Set five-year goals in these (and other) areas.

FAMILY

_____

_____

CAREER

_____

_____

HEALTH

_____

_____

FINANCES

_____

_____

EDUCATION

_____

_____

SPIRITUALITY

RELATIONSHIPS

ROMANCE

TRAVEL

ADVENTURE

CHARITY

LI

FAMILY

CAREER

HEALTH

FE

FINANCES

EDUCATION

RECREATION

RECREATION

_____

_____

CHARITY

_____

_____

ADVENTURE

_____

_____

TRAVEL

_____

_____

ROMANCE

_____

_____

RELATIONSHIPS

_____

_____

SPIRITUALITY

_____

"
IF YOU AIM AT NOTHING,
YOU WILL HIT IT EVERY TIME.
"

ZIG ZIGLAR

BE
SPECIFIC!

When you walk into a restaurant, you don't just say, "Bring me some food." Instead, you're very specific—you pick exactly what you want from the menu. Do the same for your life. Don't just say, "My goal over the next five years is to be happy." Be specific. The more clearly and vividly you visualize a goal, the easier it becomes to achieve or acquire it. If possible, ride in it, fly in it, visualize it, rehearse it, find pictures of it, and then list the steps needed to attain it.

USING VIVID DETAILS, SKETCH OR DESCRIBE

SOMETHING YOU WANT,

SOMETHING THAT WILL MAKE YOU VERY HAPPY—AN EXPERIENCE, THING, PLACE, GOAL, OR OUTCOME.

THINK
BIG.

CRAZY JUST MIGHT WORK.

**GIVE YOURSELF PERMISSION TO
AIM HIGH IN WORK AND LIFE.
TAKE TIME TO DREAM AND PLAN.**

Thinking big, blogger Kyle MacDonald started small—
with a red paper clip, to be exact. He posted it on
Craigslist and bartered a fish-shaped pen for it. Then
he traded the pen for something better. One trade led
to another, and another, until Kyle finally found himself
the new owner of a three-bedroom house.

> "MOST PEOPLE DON'T AIM
> TOO HIGH AND MISS. THEY
> AIM TOO LOW AND HIT."

BOB MOAWAD

What would you attempt if you knew you could not fail?

There isn't one person in a thousand who can write down his or her most exciting dreams without telling themselves that it's probably impossible. The truth is, virtually anything is possible—nothing is too good to be true.

WRITE DOWN A DREAM

THAT YOU WOULD LOVE TO PURSUE IF YOU ABSOLUTELY KNEW YOU COULD ATTAIN IT.

(It may be more doable than you think.)

Big doesn't have to feel big.

Big ideas can be intimidating, but even your biggest and most daunting goal can be achieved if you simply break it up into bite-sized chunks.

Struggling author Joseph Heller composed his best-selling book *Catch-22* by writing in little chunks and fitting them around his day job. Imagine what you could accomplish by applying the same principle to one or more of your biggest goals over the next five years.

Remember: the sum total of a lot of little efforts isn't little.

Don't believe everything "they" say. "They" said that Elvis Presley couldn't sing. "They" said that James Joyce couldn't write. "They" said that Michael Jordan couldn't play. Who are "they" who exercise so much power over our lives?

Remember to think for and believe in yourself.

Either you are living out someone else's dream for you, or you are setting your own course. Don't let other people tell you who you are. Form the habit of saying "yes" to your own ideas. Then write down all the reasons why they will work. There will always be plenty of people around to tell you why they *won't* work.

"...TUNE OUT THE NAYSAYERS, TUNE INTO YOUR OWN COURAGE... ONE OF MY OWN BEST MOVES IS TO SURROUND MYSELF WITH FRIENDS WHO INSTEAD OF ASKING "WHY?" ARE QUICK TO SAY "WHY NOT?" THAT ATTITUDE IS CONTAGIOUS..."

OPRAH WINFREY

Surround yourself with

PEOPLE

WHO

BELIEVE

YOU CAN.

By all means, share your goals—but only share them with people who will support you.

Here is a benchmark test: Will spending time with this person lift me up? Will he or she make me want to be a better person? A happier person? A more successful person? Will he or she help me achieve my most important goals?

LIST FIVE PEOPLE WHO CAN HELP YOU ACHIEVE YOUR DREAMS AND GOALS.

1 _____

2 _____

3 _____

4 _____

5 _____

WHY NOT YOU?

WHY NOT NOW?

DO IT NOW!

Some people spend all their lives on a boring little place called Someday Isle. "Someday, I'll be happy. Someday, I'll hike in Nepal. Someday, I'll build a log house. Someday, I'll have a great adventure." But life is not a dress rehearsal. Life is here and it is now. Reach out and seize it; you deserve it!

LIST FIVE THINGS YOU'VE BEEN PROCRASTINATING ABOUT AND

TAKE ACTION

TOWARD ALL FIVE THIS WEEK.

EACH MORNING HE STACKED
UP THE LETTERS HE'D WRITE
TOMORROW.
AND THOUGHT OF THE FOLKS
HE WOULD FILL WITH DELIGHT
TOMORROW.
IT WAS TOO BAD, INDEED,
HE WAS BUSY TODAY,
AND HADN'T A MINUTE
TO STOP ON HIS WAY;
MORE TIME HE WOULD HAVE
TO GIVE OTHERS, HE'D SAY
TOMORROW...
BUT THE FACT IS HE DIED
AND HE FADED FROM VIEW,
AND ALL THAT HE LEFT HERE
WHEN LIVING WAS THROUGH
WAS A MOUNTAIN OF THINGS
HE INTENDED TO DO
TOMORROW.

EDGAR ALBERT GUEST

TGIM!

Dreading Mondays is a ridiculous way to spend one-seventh of your life, but that's the weird habit that millions of people have fallen into.

IMAGINE THIS:

Over the next five years you'll receive the gift of about 260 different Mondays, each one coming into your life fresh and full of promise. What kind of magic and miracles could you create with that kind of time? Why not welcome every Monday with the same anticipation and excitement that most people reserve just for Fridays? Why not be a maverick?

MONDAY'S

POSSIBILIT

How can you put every Monday on a pedestal?

What if you designated every Monday as Mom Day, or Friend Day, or Family Day, or Fun Day, or...? What will make you say TGIM? Write your ideas here.

DO YOU KNOW AMAZING TRULY

HOW
YOU
ARE?

AMAZING YOU!

There has never been another you.

You are something that has never happened in history before. You are one of a kind. You are new to nature; therefore, no one can really predict to what heights you might soar. Even you will not know until you spread your wings. You may not be able to see your potential, but it's there—and it's enormous!

Your amazing instincts:

Though you may think of yourself as merely average, you are the latest in a long line of human success stories. Since the Ice Age, vast numbers of your ancestors have been smart enough, fast enough, strong enough, and courageous enough to survive several thousand years of famine, plague, predators, and the worst natural disasters. The hidden strengths you've inherited are trying their best to emerge. Let them out!

Your amazing body:

Your body has a fabulous built-in telephone system, a highly sophisticated audiovisual system, and a network of more than 60 thousand miles of blood vessels. If you laid all those blood vessels out flat, they would wrap around the circumference of the earth—twice!

Your amazing mind:

The average human brain weighs about three pounds and is made up of around 86 billion cells called neurons. Your neurons can transmit information as quickly as 120 meters per second. At those speeds, if your neurons were a car they'd be going 268 miles per hour!

Your amazing life span:

Just two hundred years ago the average American died by age 40. Today, we've nearly doubled that number. Your chances of a longer, healthier life will continue to increase well into this century. What are you going to do with your longer, healthier life?

WHAT
WILL
YOU DO
WITH
YOUR
GIFTS?

There is a much-told fable

about an elderly man who, in the final days of his life, is lying in bed alone. He awakens to see a large group of people clustered around his bed. Their faces are loving, but sad. Confused, the old man smiles weakly and whispers, "You must be my childhood friends come to say goodbye. I am so grateful."

Moving closer, the tallest figure gently grasps the old man's hand and replies, "Yes, we are your best and oldest friends, but long ago you abandoned us. For we are the unfulfilled promises of your youth. We are the unrealized hopes, dreams, and plans that you once felt deeply in your heart, but never pursued. We are the unique talents that you never refined, the special gifts that you never discovered. Old friend, we have not come to comfort you, but to die with you."

TALENT IS LIFE'S GIFT TO YOU.

WHAT YOU DO WITH IT IS YOUR GIFT BACK.

Have the courage to fulfill your potential.

If singing or dancing or math or music or leadership or sports comes easily to you, that's a gift. And if it's easy for you to be a good singer, or dancer, or athlete, why not become a great one?

List some of your natural gifts and talents. Decide you'll become great at one or more over the next five years.

HAVE
ADVEN

Take yourself by surprise: Do something that's unlike you every now and then. Escape the treadmill of predictability. Wear colored socks. Take the scenic route to work. Play Beethoven or mariachi music at your desk. Feed the birds at lunch. Give blood or visit a food bank. Plant a flaming yellow rhododendron. Buy a vegetable or fruit you've never tried before. Write a love letter to your significant other. Put down your phone and talk to other people.

Break with routine: What happened to spontaneity? At what point did you lose touch with the idea of doing something just because you felt like it in the moment—just because you're alive?

TURES.

Do something brilliant every day: Strike out in some new directions. Learn martial arts or creative dance. Make a spectacular presentation. Obliterate your sales goal. Dream a wonderful dream. Prepare an astounding meal. Tell an outrageous joke. Savor life. Remember, we only pass this way once.

SEE THE

WORLD.

WANDER & WONDER.

This is your life, your one-and-only life—shouldn't you see at least one wonder for yourself over the next five years?

Of the original Seven Wonders of the World, only the Great Pyramid of Giza still exists. But there are lots of other wonders out there to choose from. Which ones will you see for yourself?

THE SEVEN NATURAL WONDERS

GRAND CANYON
GREAT BARRIER REEF
HARBOR OF RIO DE JANEIRO
MOUNT EVEREST
NORTHERN LIGHTS
PARÍCUTIN VOLCANO
VICTORIA FALLS

THE SEVEN WONDERS OF CIVIL ENGINEERING

CHANNEL TUNNEL
CN TOWER
DELTA WORKS
EMPIRE STATE BUILDING
GOLDEN GATE BRIDGE
ITAIPU DAM
PANAMA CANAL

THE SEVEN MODERN WONDERS

ASWAN HIGH DAM
BIG BEN (ELIZABETH TOWER)
EIFFEL TOWER
GATEWAY ARCH
HOOVER DAM
MOUNT RUSHMORE NATIONAL MEMORIAL
PETRONAS TWIN TOWERS

THE SEVEN FORGOTTEN NATURAL WONDERS

ANGEL FALLS
BAY OF FUNDY
IGUAÇÚ FALLS
KRAKATOA ISLAND
MOUNT FUJI
MOUNT KILIMANJARO
NIAGARA FALLS

Circle your top destinations or make your own list.

1
2
3
4
5
6
7

I ALWAYS WA

BE IN THE STANDS AT A WORLD CUP SOCCER GAME. STAND BEHIND THE TAPE BY THE 18TH HOLE OF THE MASTERS. WELCOME THE SWALLOWS AS THEY RETURN TO CAPISTRANO. FOLLOW THE MIGRATION OF THE MONARCH BUTTERFLY. RUN WITH THE BULLS IN PAMPLONA, SPAIN. SIT ON THE GRASS AT THE MONTEREY JAZZ FESTIVAL. FEEL THE OCEAN'S SPRAY AT THE AMERICA'S CUP RACE. BE PART OF THE EXCITEMENT AN GLORY OF THE OLYMPIC GAMES. CHEER FROM THE BLEACHERS AT A WORLD SERIES GAME. BOLDLY GO AMONG THE SUPERFANS AT A STAR TREK CONVENTION. RUN WILD ON THE PLAYA AT THE BURNING MAN FESTIVAL.

NTED TO...

Attend a world-class event.

Some experiences just can't be understood any other way: you have to go to know! Make a list of your own or pull an idea from the list opposite—but make it happen.

I'm definitely going to...

VISIT THE

HOME

OF YOUR

ANCESTORS.

Who were your ancestors and how do you fit into their story?

Were they lemon farmers in Italy, olive merchants in Greece, bronze sculptors in Benin, or Buddhist priests in Tibet?

You can easily discover a lot of information about your ancestors. Simply search online for the word "ancestry" and away you go!

Whoever your ancestors were, make plans soon to go see where they came from. Walk the hills or villages where they were born. Feel their dreams, hopes, and aspirations. If possible, eat where they ate; drink where they drank; sing what they sang; sleep where they slept; pray where they prayed. You are the latest in a long family line. You deserve to see, hear, feel, taste, and touch the home of your ancestors for yourself.

"...YOU SHALL SEE WONDERS."

WILLIAM SHAKESPEARE

Anousheh Ansari always loved looking up at the stars. So when she had the opportunity to become the first female space tourist, she jumped at the chance. After returning from space to the steppes of Kazakhstan, Ansari said, "I loved being in space, and if I had a choice I would have probably stayed longer." Achieving her lifelong dream has only inspired her to keep dreaming of ways to get back up there.

TRUST
CRAZY

YOUR
IDEAS.

From the time we are in grade school,

we're taught to think that the best answers and ideas are in books or come from someone else's head. What the world really needs to know right now is what kind of dreams and crazy new ideas are in *your* head!

In 2005, three twenty-something guys wished they had a simpler method for sharing videos online with their friends. They threw together an invention—a way for virtually any video to play on any web browser—and started their own little company called YouTube. One year later, *Time* had named their idea Invention of the Year and they sold their company to Google for $1.65 billion.

WHAT IS YOUR YOUTUBE?

Many people believe they can only have one or two new ideas a year. But what if, rather than wait for ideas to come your way organically, you dedicated yourself to having one new idea every week? In five years, you'd have 250 ideas—more than most people have in a lifetime. With these odds, some of those ideas are bound to be pure genius.

WRITE DOWN YOUR WONDERFUL

IDEAS.

A single idea can transform a life, a family, a business, a nation, a world. Start here.

EVERY DAY MATTERS.

Live each day
as if it's your last…
because one day
it'll be true.

Where are you on your journey?

GET OUT YOUR PENCIL AND DO THE MATH.

1. Multiply your age x 365 days.
   (That will give you your approximate age in days.)

2. Subtract that number from 28,689 days.
   (That's an average life span these days.)

365 **x** YOUR AGE IN YEARS **=**

28,689 **–** YOUR AGE IN DAYS **=**

I probably have

days left.

WHAT YOU FOCUS ON WILL GROW.

Life is too short to be cranky:

Attitude is a choice. We create our own world by the way we choose to see it. For the next five years, your mind can focus on fear, worry, problems, negativity, and despair. Or it can focus on confidence, opportunity, solutions, optimism, and success. You decide.

Keep your word:

Say what you mean and mean what you say. Look the world straight in the eye. Live and work with honesty, openness, and integrity; keep your promises and everything else is a piece of cake.

Offer forgiveness: Forgive everyone, especially yourself. Let go of past hurts. Feelings of resentment (or revenge) are worthless—they can only drag you down. The courage to forgive and move on is liberating. Make it a rule: always be the first to forgive.

Move forward: Yesterday is a canceled check. The past is not your potential. There are good things ahead of you, and they may be greater and more wonderful than anything you've left behind. The next five years are a blank canvas—clean and bright. Why not decide to paint that canvas with rainbow colors?

Quit worrying: It's been said that 99 out of 100 things we worry about never come to pass. If you stopped worrying about what might happen tomorrow, wouldn't that give you more time to enjoy today? What did you worry about six months ago? A year ago? Five years ago? How many of your biggest worries have actually come to pass?

Be grateful: Stop and view your life through the eyes of the other seven billion people on Earth. Literally hundreds of millions of people would gladly trade places with you right now—and be ecstatic.

It's the little things: The happiness of life is made up of little things: a smile, a helping hand, a caring heart, a word of praise, a moment of shared laughter. We are most alive in those moments. Savor them all!

LOOK FOR THE SECOND RIGHT ANSWER.

Faced with a significant problem or setback, it's tempting to simply give up on your dreams or plans. Instead, try treating problems as opportunities to be creative. Realize that for every obstacle there is a solution. Discover the magic of searching for the "second right answer."

Here's an example:

Suppose you and your significant other have been planning to quit your jobs and spend the next few years exploring the highways and byways of America in your shiny new Winnebago.

Here's the problem:

Now that you're finally ready to head off into the sunset, you realize that the price of gas has skyrocketed, and you haven't saved nearly as much money as you need. What would you do? Would you give up on your dream?

Here's a second right answer:

When faced with a similar situation, Daniel and Becky Ford looked for the opportunity in their problem and found it: the Fords applied for a job as a long-haul truck-driving couple. Instead of traveling America in a Winnebago and paying for all that gas, insurance, and upkeep, they hit the road in a fully equipped 18-wheeler. Instead of tapping their savings as they had originally planned, they were actually paid to see the country.

Your resources are always far greater than you imagine them to be. Never ask, "Can I do this?" Ask instead, "How can I do this?"

Here's the principle:

Always look for the second right answer. And look closely. **What, at first, appears to be a broken dream may actually be your dream come true.**

IF YOU CAN READ THIS, THANK A TEACHER!

CELEBRATE

THOSE WHO

HELPED YOU.

Somebody saw something in you once—and that is partly why you're where you are today. **Whoever helped you along the way, find a way to thank them.**

A childhood playmate. Your first best friend. An inspiring teacher. An encouraging coach. A thoughtful neighbor. Your college roommate. A kind coworker. Your best man or maid of honor. The rabbi or minister who helped you tie the knot. The physician who delivered your baby. A caring mentor. The family member who gave you the support you needed.

Over the next five years, go back over your life and take time to thank the people who made a difference for you. A note, call, or visit from you—out of the blue—will mean the world to them. Thank them not just for what they have done for you, but for what they mean to you.

Start your thank you list on the next page today.

People I am grateful for:

"...IF YOU HAVE SOMETHING TO SAY TO A LOVED ONE, DON'T WAIT UNTIL TOMORROW. TOO LATE COMES SOONER THAN LATER."

NICK ARKON

WHEN WAS THE LAST TIME

YOU DID SOMET

FOR THE FIRST

DON'T JUST GO THROU LIFE—GRO THROUGH

T
GH
W
LIFE.

Realize that the journey of life is not about being right or pretending that you know everything—it's about learning and growing every step of the way.

Instead of getting stuck in a rut or holding yourself back, make your life an adventure. Decide today that your commitment to learning and growing over the next five years is bigger than your commitment to staying the same.

Read the great books:

Pick up Homer's *Iliad* and prepare to be amazed. See the most beautiful woman in the world, and hear the ancient clash of shields and the call of Trojan trumpets. But don't stop there. Read Leonardo da Vinci's notebooks and Cervantes' *Don Quixote* and Tolstoy's *War and Peace* and Jane Austen's *Pride and Prejudice* and Herman Melville's *Moby Dick*. You'll never be the same again!

Learn another language:

Learning a second language is a new way to see and experience the world. Learn Italian, Russian, Mandarin, American Sign Language, Farsi, or Swahili. Then get on a plane and go try it out with the people who know it best.

Master a skill:

Don't just be good, be great. Take a hobby or interest and elevate it into an art form. Learn to do something so well that people will come from miles around just to watch you do it again and again.

Become a master: What will you choose to be? A Scrabble player, a magician, a *chef de cuisine*, a ventriloquist, a ballroom dancer, a winemaker, an orchid grower, a glassblower, a martial artist, a Frisbee champ, a photographer, a stand-up comedian? The sky's the limit!

Kick a habit: If there is anything in your life that is holding you back, now is the time to think about changing it. What habits are currently preventing the best that is in you? (It can take effort to change a negative habit into a positive habit—but the benefits will last a lifetime!)

Transform negatives: What annoys you? A fast track to happiness and fulfillment is to zero in on whatever makes you unhappy, and turn those negatives into positives. Identifying what bugs you about yourself or your life is a lesson in instant clarity.

Get fit: Yoga, running, rock climbing, Hula-Hooping—it doesn't matter what you do, but do it. Get in the best shape of your life. Over the next five years give your body, your energy, and your health the attention you've always wanted to.

LIFE IS

NOW.

FORGET YOUR AGE.

It's what you do, not when you do it, that really counts.

AT AGE...

8 Mozart wrote his first symphony.

14 Country singer LeAnn Rimes won her first two Grammy Awards.

20 Debbi Fields founded the Mrs. Fields cookie company.

25 J.K. Rowling came up with the idea for Harry Potter.

45 George Foreman regained the world heavyweight title.

46 Jack Nicklaus won the Masters Tournament for the sixth time.

78 Grandma Moses made her first sale to an art collector; she was still participating in one-woman art shows well into her nineties.

84 Titian painted his famous *Allegory of the Battle of Lepanto.*

15 Swimmer Shane Gould won three Olympic gold medals.

17 Joan of Arc led an army in defense of France.

35 Martin Luther King Jr. received the Nobel Peace Prize.

43 John F. Kennedy ran for the US presidency, and won.

54 Jockey Willie Shoemaker won the Kentucky Derby for the fourth time.

62 Colonel Sanders franchised his Kentucky Fried Chicken business.

86 Ruth Rothfarb ran the Boston Marathon.

104 On his birthday, a man named Cal Evans was interviewed by a Denver reporter. "Have you lived in Denver all your life?" asked the reporter. Cal laughed and replied, "Not yet, sonny."

NEVER RETIRE! DO WHAT YOU DO AND KEEP DOING IT. BUT DON'T DO IT ON FRIDAY. TAKE FRIDAY OFF. FRIDAY, SATURDAY, AND SUNDAY, DO FISHING... THEN FROM MONDAY TO THURSDAY, DO WHAT YOU'VE BEEN DOING ALL YOUR LIFE... MY POINT IS: LIVE FULLY AND DON'T RETREAT.

MEL BROOKS

IT'S NEVER TOO LATE OR TOO EARLY.

RIGHT NOW IS A GOOD TIME.

Whether you're 5 or 105, you have a lifetime ahead of you— so renew your dreams! What are you passionate about?

What is something you've always wanted to do but haven't done?

BE THE ANSWER TO SOMEONE'S PRAYERS.

Have you heard the story of this chance meeting between two strangers? An older woman was sitting on a park bench, despondent and lonely, thinking of suicide, when a young man sat down next to her. The two of them fed the pigeons together for a few minutes. When the young man got up, he turned to the woman and thanked her for such a nice time. This seemingly small kindness restored the woman's faith in life. The young man never knew his impact and never guessed that he had saved her life.

On any given day, without really realizing it, you may be the answer to someone's prayers. If you're too busy to reach out to people in your neighborhood or community, you're too busy. **Never forget that your touch, your thoughtfulness, and your love really can work wonders in the lives of others.**

Once a week over the next five years call someone you care about. Call a lonely neighbor, or visit an elderly person in a retirement community. Take a walk. Enjoy the sun together. Eat a Popsicle. Laugh, hug, cry, or feed the birds together.

"DO YOUR LITTLE BIT OF GOOD WHERE YOU ARE; IT'S THOSE LITTLE BITS OF GOOD PUT TOGETHER THAT OVERWHELM THE WORLD."

DESMOND TUTU

HOW V

YOU CI

THE W

VILL

HANGE

ORLD?

Make a difference.

Muhammad Yunus dreamed of bringing dignity and honor to the hundreds of millions of people "all around the world who struggle every day to make a living and bring hope for a better life for their children." He started by making a "micro loan" to some basket weavers in Bangladesh. They needed to buy some tools, and they didn't want to turn to loan sharks. They had no credit, but that didn't stop Yunus and his big idea: loaning business development money to people living in poverty. The weavers thrived, and for his pioneering concept of microcredit, Yunus won the Nobel Peace Prize. The bank he founded has loaned more than $10 billion to about 7.5 million people around the world, many of them living in remote villages.

YOU ARE THE ONE YOU'VE BEEN WAITING FOR.

How do you want to change the world? There's no way too large or small.

Write down all your ideas here and then go make the world better.

You don't have to quit your job or sacrifice your family or all your free time to make a difference in the world. One person like you can change the social landscape of our country in a few hours a week. How?

"If every American donated five hours a week," writes Whoopi Goldberg, "it would equal the labor of twenty million full-time volunteers."

WHAT DO YOU CARE ABOUT?

If you think somebody should do something about it, be that somebody.

Make a list of causes you are passionate about, then get involved.

MENTOR SOMEONE.

Remember that somewhere, sometime, someone gave you a lift or an idea that started you in the right direction. Each of us can look back on someone whose simple acts of caring changed our lives—not just by teaching us, but by taking the time to be with us and to believe in us.

Decide today that you will make time in your life to mentor someone—that you will give them the gift that only you can give. Don't just give what you know, give who you are. Can't think of someone to mentor? Don't let that stop you. Just contact Big Brothers Big Sisters.

"ENCOURAGE ME, AND I WILL NOT FORGET YOU."

WILLIAM ARTHUR WARD

HOW DO YOU WANT TO BE

REMEMBERED?

The following quiz went viral online and has been answered by people all around the world. See how you do:

1   Name the five wealthiest people in the world.

2   Name the last five Heisman Trophy winners.

3   Name the last five winners of the Miss America contest.

4   Name ten people who have won the Nobel or Pulitzer Prize.

5   Name the last half dozen Academy Award winners for best actor and best actress.

6   Name the last decade's worth of World Series winners.

The point: None of us remember the headliners of yesterday. These are not second-rate achievers. They are the best in their fields. But the applause dies. Awards tarnish. Achievements are forgotten. Accolades and certificates are buried with their owners.

Here's another quiz. See how you do on this one:

1   List a few teachers who aided your journey through school.

2   Name three friends who have helped you through a difficult time.

3   Name three people who have taught you something worthwhile.

4   Think of a few people who have made you feel appreciated and special.

5   Think of three people you enjoy spending time with.

6   Name half a dozen heroes whose stories have inspired you.

Was that easier?

The lesson: The people who make a difference in your life are not the ones with the most credentials, the most money, or the most awards. They are the ones who care.

SUCCESS IS THE PROGRESSIVE
REALIZATION OF A WORTHY IDEAL.

EARL NIGHTINGALE

SUCCESS WILL NEVER BE A BIG
STEP IN THE FUTURE, SUCCESS IS A
SMALL STEP TAKEN JUST NOW.

JONATAN MÅRTENSSON

SUCCESS MEANS FEELING
PASSIONATE ABOUT WHAT YOU DO.

LINDA RODIN

SUCCESS IS LIVING UP TO YOUR
POTENTIAL. THAT'S ALL. WAKE UP
WITH A SMILE AND GO AFTER LIFE.
DON'T JUST SHOW UP AT THE GAME—
OR AT THE OFFICE. LIVE IT, ENJOY IT,
TASTE IT, SMELL IT, FEEL IT.

JOE KAPP

I HAVE MORE MONEY THAN MY
MOTHER WOULD HAVE EVER
IMAGINED, AND I STILL DON'T
JUDGE MY SUCCESS BY THAT.

URSULA BURNS

ODD AS IT SEEMS, YOU WILL
ACHIEVE THE GREATEST RESULTS IN
BUSINESS AND CAREER IF YOU DROP
THE WORD "ACHIEVEMENT" FROM
YOUR VOCABULARY AND REPLACE
IT WITH "CONTRIBUTION."

PETER DRUCKER

I AM SUCCESSFUL ON MY OWN
TERMS. BECAUSE IF YOUR
SUCCESS IS NOT ON YOUR OWN
TERMS, IF IT LOOKS GOOD TO
THE WORLD BUT DOES NOT FEEL
GOOD IN YOUR OWN HEART, IT IS
NOT SUCCESS AT ALL.

ANNA QUINDLEN

DEFINE YOUR OWN SUCCESS.

Write down your definition here.

_____

_____

_____

_____

_____

_____

_____

_____

_____

_____

_____

_____

_____

_____

_____

_____

_____

_____

_____

LIVE YOUR LIFE

so that your children can
tell their children that
you not only stood for
something wonderful—
you acted on it!

When you reach the end of your life, do you want to be one of the people who are glad they did something wonderful or one of the people who wish they'd done something wonderful?

Start doing the things today that will matter tomorrow. Don't leave this world without giving it your all. The best inheritance you can leave your kids is an example of how to live a full and meaningful life.

Close your eyes for a few minutes and imagine that today is your 100th birthday.

Your children and grandchildren are throwing a party—and a newspaper reporter has come to interview you.

What do you want to tell the reporter about your life? Your accomplishments? Your regrets? Now, open your eyes. It's not too late—you have a fresh start on life!

"I DON'T WANT TO GET TO THE END OF MY LIFE AND FIND THAT I LIVED JUST THE LENGTH OF IT. I WANT TO HAVE LIVED THE WIDTH OF IT AS WELL."

DIANE ACKERMAN

THIS IS
YOUR LIFE,

YOUR ONE-AND-ONLY LIFE.

You determine what's possible.
Ask questions, make choices,
take steps—today is the day.

THIS IS A RECORD OF YOUR TIME. THIS IS YOUR MOVIE. LIVE OUT YOUR DREAMS AND FANTASIES. WHISPER QUESTIONS TO THE SPHINX AT NIGHT. SIT FOR HOURS AT SIDEWALK CAFÉS AND DRINK WITH YOUR HEROES. MAKE PILGRIMAGES TO MOUGINS AND ABIQUIÚ. LOOK UP AND DOWN. BELIEVE IN THE UNKNOWN FOR IT IS THERE. LIVE IN MANY PLACES. LIVE WITH FLOWERS AND MUSIC AND BOOKS AND PAINTINGS AND SCULPTURE. KEEP A RECORD OF YOUR TIME. LEARN TO READ WELL. LEARN TO LISTEN AND SPEAK WELL. KNOW YOUR COUNTRY, KNOW YOUR WORLD, KNOW YOUR HISTORY, KNOW YOURSELF. TAKE CARE OF YOURSELF PHYSICALLY AND MENTALLY. YOU OWE IT TO YOURSELF. BE GOOD TO THOSE AROUND YOU. AND DO ALL OF THESE THINGS WITH PASSION. GIVE ALL THAT YOU CAN. REMEMBER, LIFE IS SHORT AND DEATH IS LONG.

FRITZ SCHOLDER

YOU WIL

HAVE

TIME TH

DO *RIGI*

. NEVER

MORE

AN YOU

IT NOW.

In loving memory of Bob Moawad.

With special thanks to the entire Compendium family.

Credits:
WRITTEN BY: *Dan Zadra and Kobi Yamada*
EDITED BY: *Kristel Wills and Ruth Austin*
DESIGNED BY: *Justine Edge*

Library of Congress Control Number: 2018955807
ISBN: 978-1-946873-55-2

1st printing. Printed in China with soy inks.

ABOUT THE AUTHORS

Dan Zadra is the CEO of Zadra Creative, and a nationally recognized author, book mentor, and strategic communications and creativity consultant. He is the much-loved founder and former Creative Director of Compendium and remains an active member of the board.

Kobi Yamada is the *New York Times* best-selling author of *What Do You Do With An Idea?* and the creator of many inspiring books. He is also the president of Compendium, a company of amazing people doing amazing things.